LET'S EXPLORE SCIENCE

Building Things

David Evans and Claudette Williams

DORLING KINDERSLEY EDUCATION
London • New York • Stuttgart

A DORLING KINDERSLEY BOOK

Project Editor Stella Love
Art Editor Sara Nunan
Designer Cheryl Telfer
Managing Editor Jane Yorke
Managing Art Editor Chris Scollen
Production Jayne Wood
Photography by Daniel Pangbourne

This is a Dorling Kindersley Education edition, 1993
0 9 8 7 6 5 4 3 2 1

First published in the United States by
Dorling Kindersley, Inc., 232 Madison Avenue
New York, 1993

Library of Congress Cataloging-in-Publication Data

Evans, David. 1937-
Building things / by David Evans and Claudette Williams. -- 1st American ed.
p. cm. -- (Let's explore science)
Includes index.
Summary: Examines, through a series of simple experiments, the different materials used to make a variety of objects.
ISBN 1-56458-344-9 (trade edition)
ISBN 0-7516-4915-5 (school edition)
1. Materials--Juvenile literature. 2. Materials--Experiments--Juvenile literature. 3. Engineering--Juvenile literature. 4. Engineering--Experiments--Juvenile literature. [1. Materials--Experiments. 2. Engineering--Experiments. 3. Experiments.]
I. Williams, Claudette. II. Title. III. Series.
TA403.2.E88 1993 93-7066
620.1'1--dc20 CIP
AC

Manufactured in Belgium

Dorling Kindersley would like to thank the following for their help in producing this book: Susanna Price (for additional photography); Coral Mula (for safety symbol artwork); Mark Richards (for jacket design); and the Franklin Delano Roosevelt School, London. Dorling Kindersley would also like to give special thanks to the following for appearing in this book: Natalie Agada; Eugenia Beaton; Marc Belsey; Karen Edwards; Sapphire Elia; Tony Locke; Paul Miller; Kim Ng; Elizabeth Robert; Daniel Sach; Anthony Singh; Nicholas Smith; and Milo Taylor.

Contents

Note to parents and teachers

Young children are forever asking questions about the things they see, touch, hear, smell, and taste. The **Let's Explore Science** series aims to foster children's natural curiosity and encourages them to use their senses to find out about science. Each book features a variety of experiments based on one topic, which draw on a young child's everyday experiences. By investigating familiar activities, such as bouncing a ball, making cookies, or clapping hands, young children will learn that science plays an important part in the world around them.

Investigative approach

Young children can only begin to understand science if they are stimulated to think and find out for themselves. For these reasons, an open-ended questioning approach is used in the **Let's Explore Science** books and, wherever possible, results of experiments are not shown. Children are encouraged to make their own scientific discoveries and to interpret them according to their own ideas. This investigative approach to learning makes science exciting and not just about acquiring "facts." This way of learning will assist children in many areas of their education.

Using the books

Before starting an experiment, check the text and pictures to ensure that you have gathered any necessary equipment. Allow children to help in this process and to suggest alternative materials to use. Once ready, it is important to let children decide how to carry out the experiment and what the result means to them. You can help by asking questions, such as, "What do you think will happen?" or "What did you do?"

Household equipment

All the experiments can be carried out easily at home. In most cases, inexpensive household objects and materials are used.

Guide to experiments

The *Guide to experiments* on pages 28-29 is intended to help parents, teachers, or helpers using this book with children. It gives an outline of the scientific principles underlying the experiments, includes useful tips for carrying out the activities, suggests alternative equipment to use, and additional activities to try.

Safe experimenting

This symbol appears next to experiments where children may require adult supervision or assistance, such as, when they are heating things or using sharp tools.

About this book

In **Building Things**, children are encouraged to experiment and investigate the properties of wood, metal, plastic, and a range of familiar objects. Children are challenged to look for similarities and differences in materials, to study their textures, strengths, flexibility, and their uses. The experiments enable children to discover that:

- matter exists in three states: solid, liquid, and gas;
- some materials can be identified by the way they look or what they feel like;
- all materials have different properties, some of which (e.g., strength, flexibility, or hardness) enable them to be used for specific purposes, such as building;
- some materials can be changed by simple processes, such as, bending, twisting, squashing, soaking in water, or rubbing;
- some materials occur naturally while others have to be manufactured from raw materials;
- some materials can be recycled (e.g., aluminum drink cans may be collected after use and the aluminum processed to be used again).

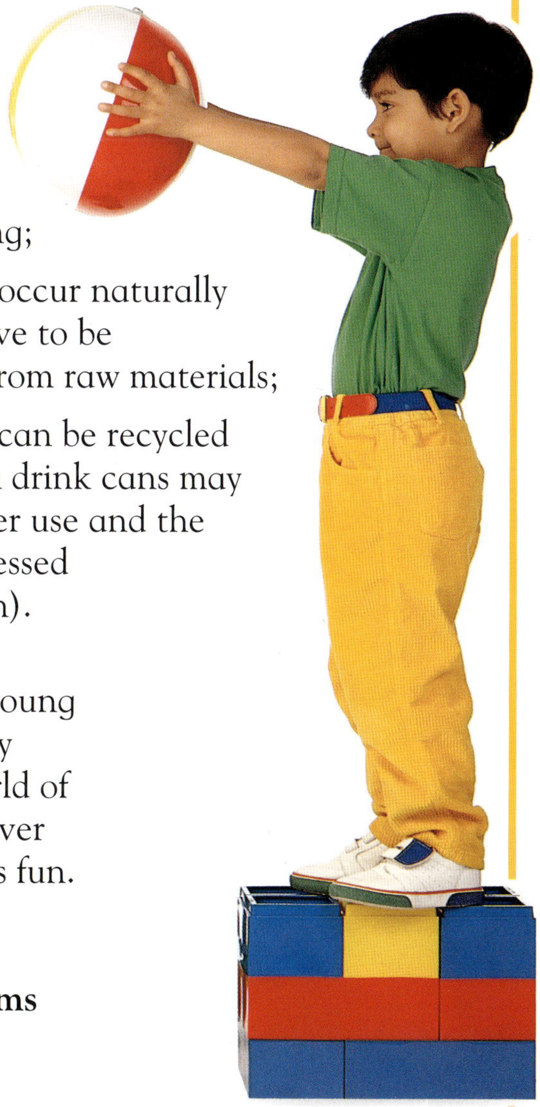

With your help, young children will enjoy exploring the world of science and discover that finding out is fun.

David Evans and Claudette Williams

What is it made of ?

Can you tell what things are made of by looking at them and feeling them?

Wood and metal
Ask a friend to help you gather lots of objects.

What kinds of things are made of wood? Close your eyes. Can you pick out all the metal objects?

What are the other objects made of?

Plastic

How many different objects can you find that are made of plastic? Are all plastics the same?

Solids, liquids, and gases

Can you find some solid things? Can you find some liquids? What things have air or other gases in them?

What is it like?

Can you study different objects and describe them?

Rough and smooth
Which objects feel rough?

Which things feel smooth? What is the smoothest thing you can find?

Shape
Can you sort some wooden blocks by shape? How else can you sort them?

Sound
What do things sound like when you tap them with a metal spoon?

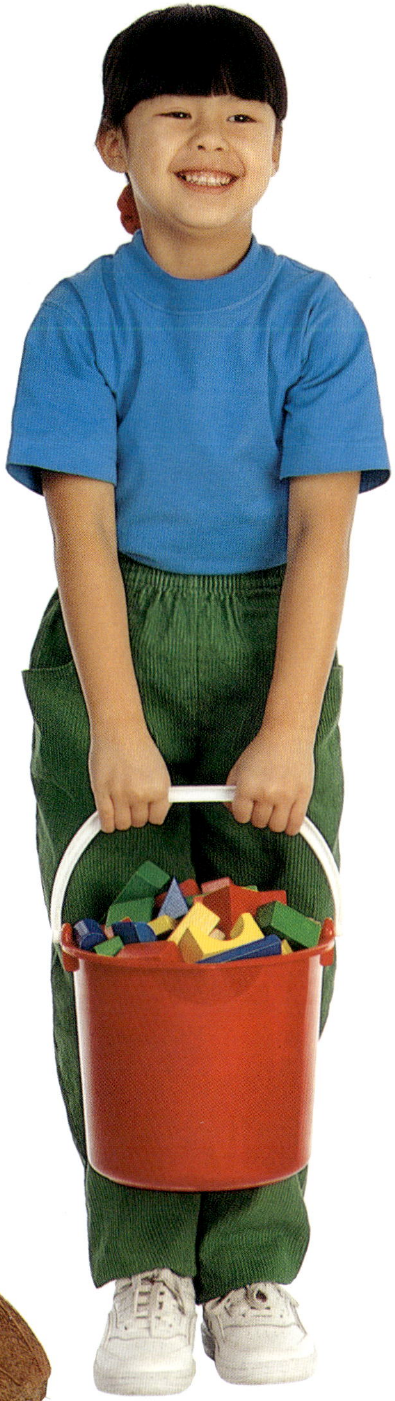

Heavy and light

Can you find some heavy things? What things are light?

What is the heaviest thing you can find?

Cold and warm

What kinds of things feel cold? Do some things feel warm?

What can you do to it?

Try these experiments on different materials to see what happens to them.

Bouncing
Can you find any of these things? Which ones bounce the highest?

Scratching

Which is the hardest thing to scratch with a nail?

Bending

Find a plastic ruler, a metal ruler, and a wooden ruler. Which one bends the most?

Feeling

Which things feel hard? Which things feel soft? What is the hardest thing you can find?

Is it strong or weak?

Can you tell which things will be strong in each experiment? Which things will be weak?

Squashing
How many bricks does it take to squash a tube? Can you squash a tube if you stand it on its end?

Folding and tearing
Find some cloth, plastic, aluminum foil, and different kinds of paper.

Which of these is hard to fold? Which one tears most easily? How many times can you fold a sheet of paper?

Breaking

Try to break some of these things. Which ones break easily? Which things are hard to break?

Twisting

What kinds of things can you twist?

Pulling

Ask a friend to help you test these materials. What will happen if you attach each thing to two sticks and pull?

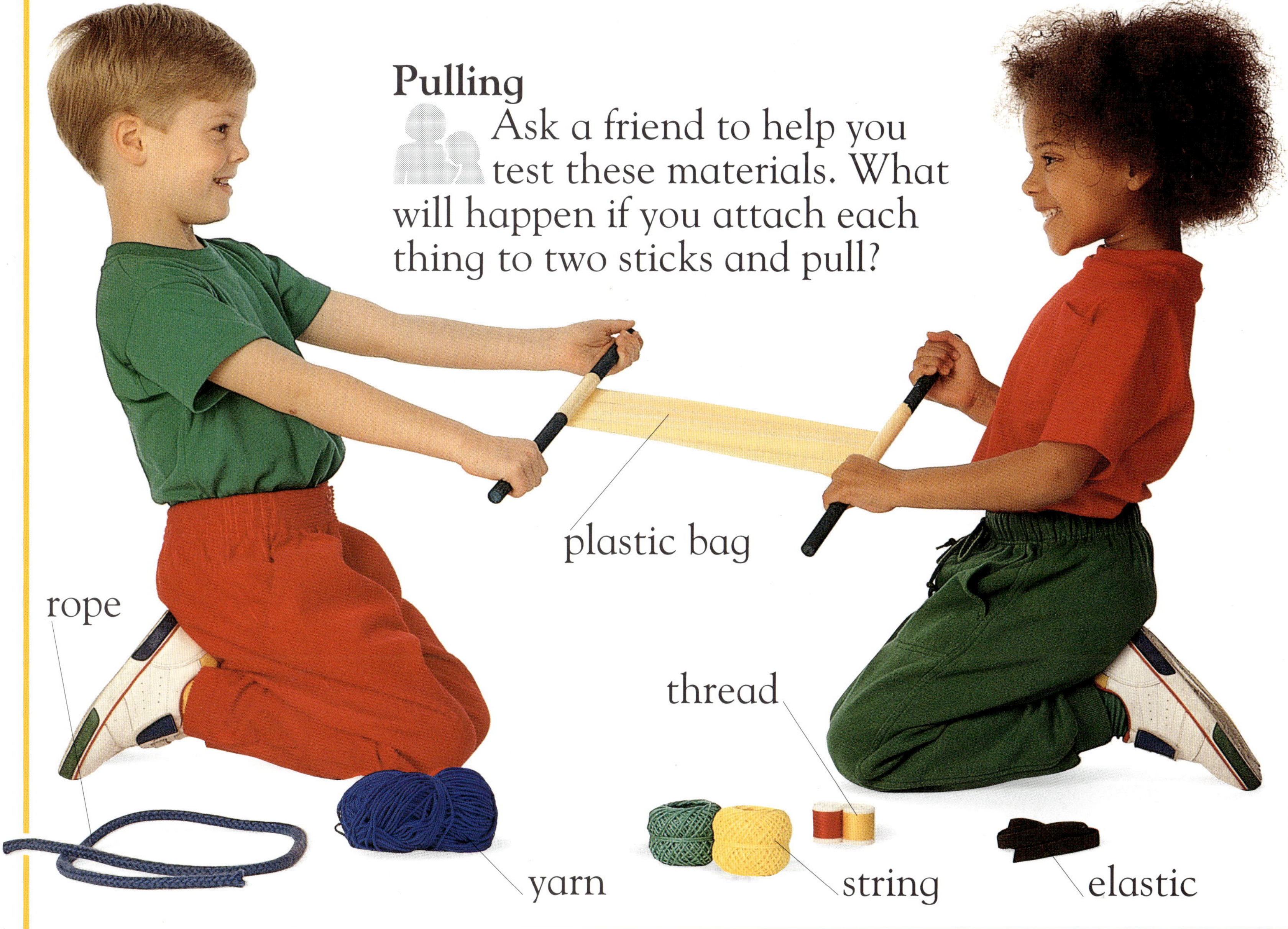

Is it made in a factory?

What kinds of things are made in a factory for us to use or eat? What kinds of things are natural and found in nature?

Natural things
How many things can you find that come from nature?

What things can you find that are made in a factory?

Food containers

Can you tell which of these foods and drinks go in which container?

What are food containers made of? Why do we put food in containers?

Which containers are thrown away after use? Which ones can be used lots of times?

Can you build things?

How many ways can you find to build towers, walls, and bridges?

Newspaper
Can you build a bridge with newspaper and tape?

Sand
Does wet or dry sand make the best sand castle?

Can you make your bridge strong enough to stand on?

Straws
Can you build a tower with drinking straws? How many straws will you use?

Plastic flowerpots
Can you build a tall tower with some flowerpots?

Building blocks
Which way of building with blocks makes the strongest wall?

Can you test your wall by rolling a ball against it?

Can you make things?

Can you make things by mixing and shaping different materials?

Always wear a dust mask when you use sandpaper or handle fine powders.

Clay bricks
Can you shape a lump of clay into a brick? Now leave it to dry.

Papier-mâché
Can you mix flour and water paste with small pieces of paper to make papier-mâché?

Take a handful of the mixture and squeeze it into a shape. Leave it to dry. What happens to it?

Plaster of paris

Can you mix plaster powder and water into a smooth paste? What happens if you pour some into a paper cup and leave it to dry?

Fiberboard

Can you make fiberboard? Mix some sawdust and wood glue together. Put some of the mixture in a paper cup and leave it to dry.

Sanding things

Can you test the materials you have made? Which is the hardest one to rub away with sandpaper?

Can you join things?

How many ways can you find to join things together?

Taping and gluing

Join together some pieces of wood or cardboard with different kinds of tape.

Can you pull the things apart? Which tape is the strongest? Now try gluing things together. Which kind of glue holds best?

Weaving
Can you use ribbons to weave a small mat?

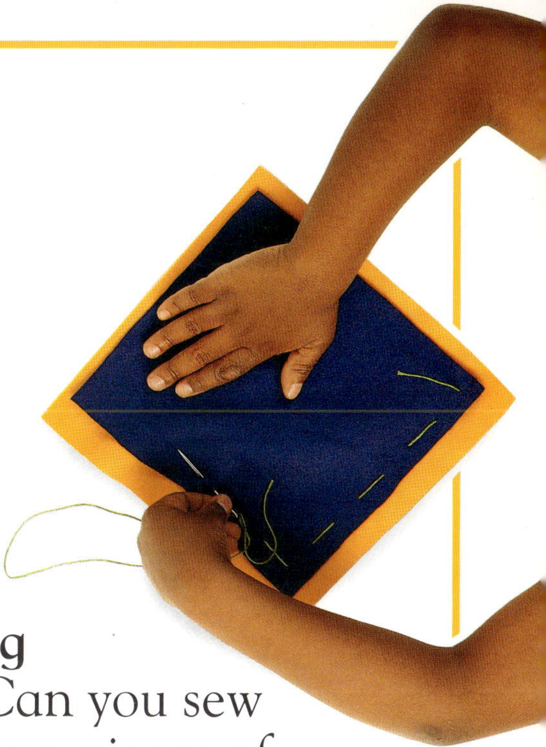

Sewing
Can you sew two pieces of cloth together? Is the seam strong? Does it make a difference if you sew with small or large stitches?

Nailing
Can you join two pieces of wood with a nail? Can you pull the wood apart again?

What happens if you use a longer nail?

Can you change things?

Try these experiments to find out if you can make things change.

Wetting
Do materials change if you make them wet?

Smoothing
Can you make rough things smooth?

Which material will be best for making an umbrella?

Painting

Can you change the color of things with paint? Which materials are hard to paint? Will adding glue to the paint make a difference?

Soaking

What will happen if you leave things to soak in water for a few days?

Index

Guide to experiments

The notes below briefly outline the scientific principles underlying the experiments and include suggestions for alternative equipment to use and activities to try.

What is it made of? 10-11

Children explore everyday objects and try to distinguish between wood, metals, plastics, and other materials. This investigation can be extended by asking questions, such as "How do you know it is made of plastic?" The idea is introduced that matter exists as solids, liquids, or gases.

What is it like? 12-13

The activities challenge children to use their senses to examine the physical properties of different materials. Additional challenges can be raised by presenting objects which are, for example, heavy and light, but made of the same material. Encourage children to describe objects in their own words after they have studied them.

What can you do to it? 14-15

These experiments extend children's knowledge of materials by asking them to find out about compressibility, flexibility, and hardness. The bouncing activity can be extended by asking children to investigate how things bounce on different surfaces, such as on a carpet or a hard floor.

Is it strong or weak? 16-17

Observing the effects of forces applied to various materials will give children some indication of the relative strength of the materials. By testing various tubes, children will discover that the tubes are stronger, i.e., harder to squash, when stood up on end. Whatever the size, thickness, or strength of the paper used, children will find that it cannot be folded in half more than eight times.

Is it made in a factory? 18-19

These activities encourage children to develop ideas about materials that occur naturally and about substances, such as plastics, that are manufactured from raw materials. By examining food wrappers and containers, children will begin to understand that certain materials are used for specific tasks because of the properties they possess. Children can be asked to think about the issues that surround throwing away or reusing materials.

Can you build things? 20-21

Here children experiment with methods of building to discover the strongest or most stable structures. The bridge can be strengthened by rolling the newspaper more tightly. Widening the base of the straw tower will give it a lower center of gravity and make it more stable.

Can you make things? 22-23

Children are asked to manufacture their own materials by combining ingredients, and molding the mixtures. Children can experiment to discover if varying the proportions of the ingredients alters the durability of the material.

Can you join things? 24-25

By joining materials together, children will learn that the strength of a structure partly depends on how its components are fixed together. Care should be taken to ensure children do not use solvent-based adhesives or those that set immediately.

Can you change things? 26-27

Children will discover that some materials are changed when soaked in water, sanded, or painted, and that some of these changes are reversible. They will also find that some materials will absorb water or paint while others are water resistant, or waterproof.